You Can't
Win
a Fight
with
Your Boss

You Can't Win a Fight with Your Boss

& 55 Other Rules for Success

TOM MARKERT

HarperCollins*Publishers*

HarperCollins*Publishers*
77–85 Fulham Palace Road,
Hammersmith, London W6 8JB
www.harpercollins.co.uk

Published by HarperCollins*Publishers* 2006
1

First published by HarperCollins*Publishers* Pty Ltd,
Sydney, Australia 2004

Copyright © Tom Markert 2004, 2006

Tom Markert asserts the moral right to
be identified as the author of this work

ISBN-10 0-00-722751-5
ISBN-13 978-0-00-722751-8

Printed and bound in Great Britain by
Clays Ltd, St Ives plc

This book is dedicated to five very important people in my life.

My parents, Tom and Monnie Markert. They gave me my values, my work ethic, and my sense of humour.

My in-laws, Anne and Bill Elwell, who allowed a snot-nosed kid to marry their daughter and then proceeded to treat me like another son. Sadly my father-in-law, Bill, passed away after a fight with cancer, but he will always be remembered as an awesome man. I learned a lot from you, Bill!

And most importantly, my wife, Sarah. She is the cornerstone of our family. With my travel schedule and job requirements, it could not work without her. Plain and simple.

CONTENTS

INTRODUCTION

'A journey of a thousand miles must begin with a single step.'

Chinese philosopher Lao-tzu said this during the sixth century B.C. It is fantastic advice, and it has lived through the ages. The fact that you are reading this book – taking a single step – means you will have an advantage over your competitors.

You can learn from the past as well as from others, and certainly from your own successes and failures. The process of learning will accelerate your path to correct action, and taking correct action is what will get you ahead inside companies of any size at a faster pace.

Working your way up inside a company can be a

great adventure, even a wild ride. There is no magic formula to ensure success, but there are some black-and-white rules you must follow if you want to get to the top. I have drawn upon my twenty years of experience with companies such as Procter & Gamble, Citicorp, and most recently information giant ACNielsen, to write the rules that I hope will help to propel you to the top. So, if you are willing to learn, read on!

If you think you already know everything you need to know in order to achieve career success, I applaud your ego, but watch out – because you're about to be mown down by someone who is playing by a set of rules you don't even know about. That's a guarantee. It happens every day inside every company.

Follow these rules and you might just get to that corner office; ignore them and you might just end up as roadkill – lying dead by the side of the corporate highway as others drive right past you.

Whether you are a recent graduate just entering the workforce or already in the corporate game, the ninety minutes or so it will take you to soak up the learning in this book will be some of the best time you have ever spent.

Open your mind, read with passion, and *learn*.

RULE 1

Work Hard and Smart

If you hear the words *get rich quick*, run for the hills. You are being scammed.

To make money, you have to work. To make lots of money, you have to work really hard and really smart.

Rule 1 is the cornerstone of this book: Remember, work hard and smart.

RULE 2

No One Is Entitled
to Anything!

Hear this now. No one inside a company is entitled to anything. Not one thing. Not ever.

If you think you are entitled to keep your job, you are not.

If you think you are entitled to a promotion, you are not.

If you think you are entitled to more money, you are not.

If you think you are entitled to a big office, you are not.

Business has nothing to do with entitlement. Business is about achievement. If you consistently deliver the goods, your rewards will come.

I am not in favour of staff programmes that

reward seniority. The stakes for a new employee should be the same as those for a long-term employee. You deliver, you move ahead. You also get paid more.

I take a similar position with tenure. In some countries, for instance, teachers have a job for life once they survive a tenure period. That's crap! I couldn't care less about tenure. Under tenure arrangements, employees can coast. No way. That will never be allowed in a successful company.

If you don't perform, you can't keep your job!

RULE 3

Be Motivated

You can't become a senior executive inside a large company today if you do not have a robust ego. The work that it takes to drive success at the elite level is too tough, too complex and too demanding for a person who is not somewhat egocentric to survive.

Your ego can drive in you a *need* to achieve results and a blinding fear of failure. Every senior executive position is highly visible. It is no different from being the coach of any sporting team in the world today. Emmett Davis, head coach of men's basketball at Colgate University, once told me: 'My results are in the newspaper every day.' These comments were echoed by Australian Olympic basketball coach and Sydney Kings boss Brian

Goorjian: 'Everyone knows how my day in the office was. It was on radio and TV.' It's the same inside a company, where the scorecard is the annual report – and lots of people read it. Coaches and managers with losing records don't get to keep their jobs. Fear motivates.

Money also motivates. You can make plenty of money at the top of many large companies. The salary packages that are offered are often massive, because the impact an executive has on an organization is likewise massive – good or bad. Companies pay for both talent and performance. If money is a motivator for you – fantastic, you have a shot at moving up quickly.

If you are looking for a rewarding career that does not involve huge money, you can choose many professions that compensate you with 'psychological income'. For example, social workers are usually unsung heroes; they help people resolve enormous problems, their work is usually very difficult, yet they make very little money. However, they do get the opportunity to make a difference in people's lives, which can be hugely rewarding. That said, psychological income does not motivate people who want to run big companies.

Ego and money can be good. Let's not pretend otherwise.

RULE 4

Put in the Hours

You can't cheat the clock. You are not going to get ahead without a very major commitment to your job in terms of pure hours. I have worked all over the world over the past twenty years and have found this to be universally true. Some cultures require more than others. North America is the toughest. Ted Marzilli, vice president of corporate development of VNU, recalls his early days at a top consulting firm in the United States.

'We used to laugh when we had to complete a timesheet – the maximum we could bill per week was forty hours (eight hours per day) – whereas in reality there were weeks when that forty-hour total we wrote down represented only half of the hours we spent at work. But that was the environment; we had to deliver for our clients and you, personally, had to maintain your internal reputation. Time spent on the job was certainly not the only measure of performance, but if the team was ordering a dinner delivery at 8 P.M., and you said, "No thanks, I plan to leave shortly," well, you could only get away with that once in a while, and your teammates certainly took notice. Leaving "early" was definitely not the typical path to success.

'There is no shortage of work to be done on any consulting project. It's a rare occasion when your project manager or project partner might say, "Gee, you have been working too hard lately, why don't you leave early tonight?" The environment is up or out – if you do not perform, you will be asked to leave the firm. You are always under pressure to perform, regardless of how senior you are in a company; every project is a new "proving" ground. You can never rest on your laurels.'

Whether it's by recording billable hours or setting up an environment where long hours are the expectation, professional service firms use time spent at work as an important way to measure an individual's commitment and contribution. And it isn't just about the number of hours; it's about squeezing every bit of productivity possible out of every minute of the day. And you can forget lunch breaks. You can't make money for a company while you're eating lunch.

If you don't put in the hours, someone just as smart and just as clever as you will. Fact of life: The strong survive. My own policy is to avoid working weekends. Frankly, it is good to get the break, but sometimes it can't be helped. I've always allowed the company to really own me from Monday to Friday. I pound out the hours: never less than sixty a week, and sometimes way more. But I've always said, 'Preserve the weekend.' You won't perform well if you work *all* the time. It is important to stay fresh. Work like a dog during the week, but try not to work at all at weekends. You need two days to rest, relax and have fun. You will be more productive when you are working if you have had a break.

Preserving the weekends is not as easy as it sounds – it's very easy for one or two work tasks to really encroach on your free time. I always tell my co-workers that I don't check e-mail or voicemail at the weekends, and pretty soon they realize I mean it.

You do need to be prudent, though: Sometimes there will be an emergency and you will need to work – just ensure that you make working at the weekends a rare exception to your usual rule. Your body and brain need to rest so they can perform on game days.

But talent without major commitment won't get you to the top. As you work your way up in any organization, there will always be lots and lots of equally talented executives. The tie always goes to the harder worker.

Find out who is in the office before and after you. Take a walk around early and late in the day. Those who are working harder than everyone else consistently are chasing the title. They are your competition.

I can tell you, having been the CEO of several companies, I have always made a habit of walking around early and late to personally see who's pumping it out. If they are getting results and working harder than everyone else, I promote them. They are the 'Rock Stars' – the money players.

Couples who are trying to balance serious careers with raising a family have to consider how they can put in the hours needed while caring for their children. I have seen it work, and I have seen it fail. Quite simply: it works when you have a very flexible childcare situation; it fails when you don't. You have to be available for last-minute meetings with the CEO that may run over time. You can't go running out the door at 5 P.M. if your work isn't done. If you are determined to maintain your career at the elite level, pay the money to have a flexible and high-quality childcare situation. Lots of couples do it. You can, too.

Criteria for promotions inside companies are often thought to be black-and-white. Candidates who get promoted are often thought of as the perfect choice. Nothing could be further from the truth. Choices are muddy and difficult. In fact, sometimes the person who gets promoted is simply the least objectionable candidate. Honest, that happens!

No matter what your job is, do it a little

harder and a little longer each and every day. Finish an extra report, call on one more customer, ask one more question . . . set yourself apart.

RULE 5

Do Whatever It Takes

James Carville, a political strategist, perfectly summed up what it takes to succeed on a winning team during an appearance on *The Tonight Show with Jay Leno.*

Carville explained to Leno that whenever he is interviewing a prospective candidate, if he or she says they won't 'suck up' to get ahead, the interview is over. He wants people on his team who are prepared to do whatever it takes to win.

Succeeding often means you have to be a chameleon. It doesn't mean being dishonest or false; it does mean finding a legitimate way to achieve your goals. Sometimes it requires you to do things that are uncomfortable or unnatural to you. Stretch out and go for it. Don't compromise your values, but find a way to win.

If you can't make that total and complete commitment to winning, you won't make it to the top; too many others – your competition – do have that drive and desire. Dig deep and see if you have it.

A friend of mine, Andrew Michael, works in the clothing business. He told me how he was once desperate to meet the then new managing director of a leading department store, Dawn Robertson. Frustrated after several attempts, he phoned her assistant and literally begged for an appointment, but to no avail. He then asked the assistant when Dawn's next flight was, and said: 'I don't care where or when, ask her if I can sit next to her.' They took a flight together and the rest is history. Dawn thought Andrew was crazy but liked his persistence. They both laugh about the story now and have continued to do business together. A flight to nowhere can lead to somewhere!

RULE 6

Be Charming

In business you are always selling: sometimes to external customers, sometimes to internal employees. When you leave home in the morning, turn on your charm. Be upbeat, be happy, smile, be interesting and be helpful.

Successful people sell themselves every minute of every day. This doesn't mean you should come across as a slick salesperson, smarmy or insincere. The trick is to simply be sincere *and* charming. It is not terribly hard to do – it should just come naturally to most people.

RULE 7

Find Good Bosses

Look closely at the leadership above you and try to find a great boss to work for. It's no different from when you attended college or university. Think back. There were great teachers and ordinary teachers. Who did you learn the most from? Who made learning fun? It's the same thing inside a corporation.

I was once lucky enough to be able to work for an absolutely awesome boss. He offered me the job of president of ACNielsen Canada, and at the time it was a big, big job for me. His name was Maury Pagés and he was a gentleman in every sense of the word. He came to ACNielsen after a long and hugely successful career with Pepsi.

What made my experience with him memorable was that he always made me feel confident and energized. He was always positive. He let me run my business, but of course he yelled at me at all the right times! And he was always there. If I needed him on the phone, I got him. If I needed him in Canada, he came. If I needed him at a client meeting, again, he always came. He cared about my family and we shared a love of basketball. I ran through mountains for that man. I had never worked harder and never been happier. He found the way to really motivate me!

Good bosses are hard to find, but they do make a huge difference. If you have the choice, pick the best boss.

RULE 8

Respect Your Boss

Your boss is your meal ticket, and you must treat him or her with respect. You must help your boss to succeed and to look good.

Your respect for your boss needs to be sincere. Any outward sign of disrespect will look to others in the corporation like mutiny. Would you hire or promote someone capable of mutiny? You wouldn't, because you'd be spending half your time looking over your shoulder.

This may seem obvious, but it continually happens inside corporations and the results are always the same: the boss wins, the mutinous employee loses. If the employee involved is lucky, he or she may just be shuffled to a different department under a new manager, but it can result in his or her name being added to a redundancy list.

Bosses come in all sizes, shapes and flavours. Some you will like and some you will not, but that is irrelevant. They are your conduit to moving forward, and without their support you are stuck.

Always be calm and in control with your superiors. Never withhold any information from them. With the exception of Christmas, bosses hate surprises. Surprises in business can be a disaster. Surprises make managers look out of touch and out of control.

If you think bad news is coming, tell your boss. Position things carefully, but get the truth out. Bad news can be dealt with very effectively in a big or small company with a bit of planning and time. Avoid a crisis at all costs.

Offer advice to your boss in a polite and respectful manner. Don't try to step on his or her territory. If you are open with your boss, generally he or she will be open with you. Your boss has information that you will need to be successful, and if he or she steps on your air hose . . . well.

The quickest way to get ahead is to get your boss promoted. Make your boss look good at every opportunity. Make non-threatening suggestions when you see things that are not quite right. Clear the way for your boss's success, because your boss's success can be *your* success.

Remember: your boss has conversations with his or her boss about *your* career and progress. A couple of carefully chosen words from your boss can push you forward or stop you dead in your tracks.

The most important person in your career is your boss – never forget that.

RULE 9

You Can't Win a Fight with Your Boss

A very quick way to destroy your career is to pick a fight with your boss. It is a fight you cannot win under any circumstances, so why bother?

You can only push a discussion with your boss to a certain point before it will turn into a heated debate and then a fight. You will each land verbal blows, and even if you agree to disagree, trust me, your boss will never forget it.

People have disagreements inside corporations all the time. Disagreement and debate is a healthy exercise that usually helps companies and individuals reach correct decisions. Accept that you will have many debates with your boss during your career. Debate all you want, but don't let the debate escalate into a fight. Once you cross that line you can never come back – regardless of whether or not you were right. You will be perceived as being immature and disrespectful, as well as untrustworthy and disloyal. Emotional outbursts and tantrums are taboo inside companies. If you lose your cool, you will kill your career.

Learn to compromise – or, rather, to align with your boss's decisions. Your boss will always wield a bigger stick than you do. It's fine to make your points, but always accept your boss's final call and move on. You will live to fight another day, and maybe one day you will be the boss.

You should also learn the 'emotional elasticity' of your boss. In simple terms, how far can you stretch your boss until he or she will snap?

A few years back I watched in horror during a meeting in which a colleague of mine had a fight with her boss. There were seven or eight of us in attendance, and every minute or so the debate between the two heated up to a new level. Several of us tried to jump in, but to no avail. Finally, the boss just snapped. He shouted at her and she shouted back. Up until that point the argument seemed trivial, but all of a sudden the tension in the room was indescribable. Her career with the company ended at that point. She was moved to another manager as 'damaged goods'. Eventually she left and had to start her career again elsewhere. I caught up with her recently and asked her about that fight. She admitted, looking back on it now, that she had been stupid: the issue was small in the scheme of things and she should never have allowed the argument to happen. She deeply regretted the incident and was clearly still scarred by what had occurred that day and its consequences.

You Can't Win a Fight with Your Boss.

RULE 10

Know Your Boss

What is the best way to keep your boss informed? You should know the answer to this question. Every boss is unique, and every boss responds to certain things in a different way.

If I have an important issue for my boss, would he or she prefer a short e-mail, a phone call, a voicemail – or some combination? If you don't know, find out. The first rule of communicating effectively with your boss is: give it to them the way they want it.

How much do you know about your boss? Are you making your boss's life easier?

I have a short attention span, so if my colleagues want something from me they need to get to the point really fast. This includes conversations, presentations, e-mails and voicemails. I do not have a technical background, so colleagues also need to 'dumb down' any conversations about technology. I hate getting calls at the weekend. I hate traveling on a Sunday. I don't like eating fish. I don't like late dinners. I don't fit into small cars. . .

The point is, you need to collect as much knowledge about your boss as possible and do things that make him or her most comfortable. It's just plain smart. Treat your boss as you would an important client. Win your boss over every day and on every encounter. If you don't, somebody else will.

RULE 11

Stay on the Right Side of the Boss's Spouse

Never underestimate the importance of being on the right side of the boss's spouse or partner. He or she can be as deadly to your career as your most bitter enemy.

You will almost certainly have a few opportunities to interact with your boss's spouse or partner, and you must make a good impression every time. A good outcome is good, a neutral outcome is okay, but a poor outcome means you can bet he or she will give the boss an earful on the drive home.

Present the appropriate image. Maintain your professionalism and be warm and friendly. Try to avoid work topics whenever possible. Do not be confrontational – at all costs. If you sense things are not going as well as you would like, excuse yourself and move on. Remember, a neutral outcome is okay!

The reason I know this rule so well is that I always receive a commentary from my wife during the car ride home after a work function. Frankly, I really like it. She is a very good judge of people, and over the years I have heard it all: he was drunk; she was rude; he's having an affair; he forgot my name . . . the list goes on. Treat your boss's spouse or partner as you would a senior executive. Be prepared, and be on your best behaviour.

RULE 12

Look the Part

Before you leave for work today, take a really good look in the mirror and ask yourself if you look like a CEO. If your answer is 'No,' or 'I'm not sure,' or, God forbid, 'I don't care because you don't get ahead based on looks,' you have an immediate problem that you must decide to overcome.

The way you dress is an opportunity for you to send a clear message to those who will judge your ability to move up. If you don't look the part, you won't get the part. Dressing has become more complex with the advent of business-casual clothing. You now need an informal and formal wardrobe. Look at your clothes as a very necessary investment. Spend money on the right labels – *always* look sharp.

Consciously try to overdress and, most of all, think navy blue. Man or woman, you must own at least one navy-blue 'killer suit' of the highest quality, with a white shirt or blouse and complementary shoes. Strap on a quality wristwatch (it won't be cheap). Buy a classic – the kind with a gold-and-silver wristband so it will go with any belt or pair of shoes. Add a nice pen like a Waterman or MontBlanc (reasonably priced at most office supply stores) and you are ready. That is what you should wear and carry for every meeting with senior executives. Visual impressions are lasting impressions. Get it right.

Now for an embarrassing confession. Early in my career, I struggled when it came to wardrobe considerations. Of course I didn't know it at the time, but I was lucky enough to have a manager who not so subtly set me straight. This manager summoned me to his office and told me to sit down. He had a very nice clothing catalogue lying open on his desk. He picked up his phone and proceeded to order six suits with the phone on speaker. As he was finishing up, he leaned over to me and said, 'You should order this blue one.' Not wanting to offend him, I did so. At the time, considering my salary, it was a big investment. About an hour later it hit me like a brick: his calling me in to his office while he was ordering his suits was no coincidence. It was a clear message. I was wearing the wrong battle gear!

By the way, he is the best executive recruiter in the United States today, and his name is John O'Keefe.

Let's go a step further and tackle an even more controversial area. In most Fortune 1000 companies facial hair is *out*. If you have to wear it, wear it at your own peril – and make sure it is neat and trimmed. Can you name five CEOs who have a beard?

In big companies CEOs *must* project a confident and clean image. There could be some Freudian thing to it – about hiding behind facial hair – but the truth is that very few senior executives have facial hair.

Go with the odds here and shave cleanly.

Obviously facial hair is a non-issue for women, but you don't escape the general principle here. Make sure your hair is always tidy and that it *never* covers your face. If you go to the gym in the mornings, do your hair before you arrive at work. Don't turn up with wet or messy hair. It looks sloppy and unprofessional. Make the time to ensure that you look your best when you turn up at the office. It is critical that you always look the part.

RULE 13

Smile, It's Infectious

Smile whenever you can! Smiling is infectious. Laughing is infectious. That's why the major film studios pump laughter tracks into TV sitcoms.

During interviews with potential employees, I always look to see whether they smile and laugh. Their body language often communicates as much to me as their dialogue. The energy they convey during the interview is usually indicative of what you will get from them when they work for you. As I mention elsewhere in this book, there are lots and lots of skilled people in the world. Give me happy, energetic *and* the right skills. Good managers smile all the time!

Laughing and smiling have a place inside all

companies. People notice and respect those who are confident and in control. Happy people are people who are in control. You get more out of a happy workforce than you do out of a miserable workforce. The small things always count, and the easiest thing in the world to produce is a smile.

RULE 14

Stay Healthy

I am a recent convert to eating well. I'm still not perfect – and never will be – but you can't argue against the benefits of a balanced diet. Life is meant to be enjoyed, though; all you've got to do is strike a balance. Cheeseburgers are okay once in a while if I am eating fruit, vegetables and other lower-fat items at other times. Try to eat sensibly *most* of the time. This is important, so invest time in reading up on it. Talk to your doctor or a dietician. It is worth spending some money to get professional advice on creating your own diet plan. Remember to write down your goals. Pretty soon you will feel the results.

Travelling takes its toll and you have to be careful. Aeroplane food is universally terrible.

Some people pack their own healthy snacks – a great idea. Time, of course, is the enemy on the road – translation: fast food. Be conscious of what you are eating and ask yourself if you are eating reasonably well. If you don't know, that's a problem, and you need to resolve this with better information.

When I am not eating well, my energy levels fall and work becomes harder.

In conjunction with eating right, you must get a reasonable amount of exercise. I am not a fan of diets. I don't think it's healthy to lose lots of weight and then put it back on as soon as you stop dieting. It's better to get to the right weight and then work at maintaining it. It's not really hard to eat right, so don't make lazy excuses.

Remember, food is fuel. Fuel is an element of performance. Bad fuel means low performance.

I work out three times a week, without fail. It doesn't matter what exercise I do, as long as I sweat for forty-five minutes.

Stress and tension flee the body during a solid workout. If you travel, almost every hotel has a gym. If you are a morning person, go in the morning. I'm not, so I go in the evening. Treat it as a commitment you can't break. Schedule your workout sessions in your calendar. Be proud of it. Get a colleague or friend to join you – having a buddy will keep you motivated.

For me, the two simplest forms of exercise are running and walking. All I need are shorts, a T-shirt and trainers. I can do this anytime, anywhere, and on a moment's notice. Talk to your doctor or visit your local gym to find out what exercise programme will be best for you.

Exercise is no fun until you get in shape, so be patient. Once you have established a regular routine, you will sleep better at night and you will perform better during the day. You will have strength when others tire. You will be buoyant when others are grumpy. You will look sharper and finish stronger.

The best advice on keeping fit I have ever received came from my first days on the job with a company that insisted all employees pass a company physical examination. After completing my exam (I passed, by the way), the elderly doctor said to me: 'Son, I want you to promise me two things. First, always take the stairs and not the lift, and second, always park your car in a spot that is a long way from the door.' I promised, and have been true to my word. Think about even the most simple ways you can add to your fitness regime. Every bit helps. The doc was right!

RULE 15

Become an Expert

Think about your job and figure out an area or two where you could gain an advantage by being more knowledgeable, then read everything you can about the subject. Be resourceful.

Years ago I accepted a job with a company at a time when it was attempting to launch a card-based shopper-loyalty programme. Being new to the company, I sat quietly in a cross-department meeting, listening to individuals discussing what would and wouldn't work; I was unsure about what was fact and what was fiction. One thing I realized is that I had better damn well know what had worked and what had failed in the past. After that meeting, my team and I spent two days dissecting every piece of information we could find about loyalty schemes around the world. At the next meeting, I felt like a Cheshire cat: I knew more than anyone else in the room. No one could try to fool me. Those two 'investment' days were fun for me and great for the company.

It is rewarding (and fun) to walk into a meeting as the expert. You will awe your audience, and your career star will shine more brightly.

RULE 16

Read Books

A wise man once told me that it is easy to become an expert on almost any topic. He said all you have to do is read five books on any subject and bang, you know it all. In general, it is pretty good, albeit simple, advice.

Great things are written and said every day. The challenge is, first of all, to find them and then to absorb them. Get to a bookshop twice a month and buy a couple of books from hot authors, professors or business leaders. These books are jammed with ideas that you can apply to your life and company. Even if you don't agree with all the messages in a book, the process will at least force you to open your mind to something different. Search for nuggets of gold.

If you are wondering what to read, I would focus on anything business-oriented that makes it on to the *Times* best-seller list. I like reading things by authors who are running or have run big companies: *Winning* by Jack Welch, for example, the former chairman and CEO of General Electric. To read about someone who has run a big company successfully and with so much competition is just magic: you can learn *so* much.

Most CEOs read a lot of books because they are constantly in search of the next big trend or the next big idea. They didn't make it to the corner office just because of their good looks!

RULE 17

Get an MBA

I don't have one and I wish I did. The reason
why is very simple. It is a differentiator. You get
an extra point beside your name inside a big
company if you have one. You can still succeed
without one, but you can certainly succeed a bit
more easily with it. Generally, the question
'Does he/she have an MBA?' comes up at promotion time. If two candidates vying for a job
are equal in talent and experience but one has
an MBA, the MBA will win.

In America, MBAs from the most prestigious schools become merchandised inside
many companies. Being able to drop a comment about being a 'Harvard MBA' lends an
aura of great intelligence and learning that a
smart manager can leverage internally.

It is probably best to have a couple of years of work experience before you start studying for your MBA, but the point is to get it any way you can and at the best school you can manage.

Don't let money hold you back from getting an MBA. Many corporations will subsidize continuing education for their employees. Approach your boss and see if your company would be willing to help out in any way. When I was working in Boston, I had a very bright, high-flying employee who approached me with a detailed presentation on why the company should consider helping with her MBA efforts. It was outside of company policy to do this, but I was impressed, so I put her proposal forward and the company approved it. I felt sure that both she and the company would prosper under the arrangement. In the end we all won!

Don't be afraid to ask. You can also consider spreading out the duration and costs of obtaining an MBA. It doesn't matter if it takes you two years or five – stop making excuses and just get it done. By the way, lots of people are doing it over the internet now.

Additionally, you should constantly encourage

those who work for you to pursue further education. Trust me, you will meet massive resistance on this one. Everyone mouths the words about how important training is, yet when it is time to actually get the training, all the excuses come out of the book. You will hear 'I don't have time,' 'It is a waste of time,' 'I'll do it next time,' and some that are even more creative. Ignore the excuses and tell them to make it happen.

Training and education on every level create better people. Better people get better results. You are paid to get results. So, all the logic is there!

Classroom training is fine, but so is simply attending business lunches. New thinking can come in any form. Let your people know how important personal development and training are to your organization. Quiz staff regularly about what they've done recently to improve their education. Ask them for specific details and compliment them for their extra efforts. They will quickly realize that training is not optional!

If you are at the beginning of your career and looking for new opportunities, take a moment to give yourself an honest assessment of your own skill set. Are you a good listener? Are you a good salesperson? Do you build relationships quickly? Are you a good problem solver? Everyone has areas they can improve on, and there is no shame in getting the education or practice necessary to do just that. Identify an area you want to improve in and then find a course that matches your need. Put together a description of the course as well as the costs involved and then sit down and talk to your boss about it. If your request is reasonable, you will succeed.

One final thing: After you have completed your course, circle back with your boss and let him or her know how it went, including a couple of key things you have learned. Make sure you say thank you for the training opportunity and the personal support. And, importantly, find a way to incorporate your new learning into doing your job better. If you can't do this, you have wasted your time and the company's money.

RULE 18

Write Well

I learned to write well and now I consider it a gift. Written communication is very important. Every bit as important as personal communication.

This hit home for me when I was twenty-six. At the time I was an account executive at ACNielsen in New York. We were trying to win a large contract with a huge consumer-products company. I had heard that the CEO of our parent company was an acquaintance of the president of the company we were trying to win over. With permission from my boss, I sent a carefully crafted one-page letter to the CEO, summarizing the situation and asking for his help. Scared to death, I couriered the note to his office. Two hours later, he phoned me directly and told me to come – immediately – to his office. I ran the five blocks, filled with a mixture of fear and excitement. Upon arrival, I was ushered into his palatial office. He shook my hand and told me it was the best damn note he had ever received. I remember he said: 'It's simple and I get it.' He asked a few questions, dismissed me, made a call to the company we were trying to win over, and we landed the business!

The point is, be smart with letters and e-mails. Ruthlessly consolidate and organize your messages. As a rule, if you can't say what you want to say on one page, it probably isn't worth saying – and you may do more harm than good. Present the facts and make sure the reader knows exactly what you recommend and what he or she needs to do.

And yes, I complimented this CEO's critical contribution in every speech I made about the sale. I am not stupid. I often wonder what he said about his contribution to his boss . . . the board of directors. I bet I know!

RULE 19

Know Your Numbers

If you are an English major like me (without an MBA), admit that you need help with maths! You *must* learn to read and understand basic financial reporting. Financial reporting is paramount in publicly traded companies. The financials are the most important thing a CEO reads every month.

There is an old saying, 'The numbers never lie' – and they don't! Executives must know their numbers inside and out. You must always be ready to answer questions or defend your position regarding the financials.

If you need help, ask for it. It is not complicated, and it is critical to your success. This is an area that causes the undoing of CEOs and managers who are either simply too lazy to dig around and find the facts or too stupid to acknowledge their own weakness in understanding financials.

Don't become an ostrich. Burying your head is not a good strategy in business.

Find a Mentor

Everybody needs a mentor in business. A mentor is someone you can talk to about anything in your business life, someone you can bounce ideas off, someone who can set you straight when you lose the plot (it is inevitable that you will do this occasionally), someone who truly cares about your career, and someone you can trust. A mentor can provide a safe haven. Your mentor should be someone older than you who has far more experience in business than you do.

Bob Livingston is my mentor. Bob is now semi-retired, but he seems busier than ever. Bob was the vice president of sales for Lipton Tea for many years and is now involved in marketing consulting in Hollywood. He was briefly my boss at ACNielsen.

Bob is my go-to guy, and I seek his advice often. I trust him completely – he always tells me the truth, even if it annoys me. If I am not sure about something, I take five and call him; other times I just call to check in. I always know he is there for me. He has helped me avoid mistakes because he has been around the block more often than me.

I have two people who use me as their official mentor and I love it. It makes me a better manager, and it's rewarding and fun to help someone with their career.

Find a mentor. We all need one.

Also, when the time is right, become a mentor: you've got to give if you want to take.

RULE 21

Start and End Meetings on Time

Sounds simple, right? Wrong. Badly run meetings are one of the low points of business today. People schedule meetings all the time. Some are worthwhile, most are not. Often they are just an excuse to avoid making a decision.

If you have to have a meeting, and it's your meeting, you need to do all of these things:

- **Create an agenda.**
- **Make sure attendees know what you want them to contribute.**
- **Allocate a specific amount of time on the agenda for every item.**
- **Run the meeting according to a timed schedule.**

- **Follow up with a written summary after the meeting, including required action items and who is responsible for each.**

My meetings start and end on time. We only discuss important items – if we do get off track, it is never for long. In today's environment of consensual management, the sheer number of meetings has exploded – a woeful trend. Minimize the number of meetings you have and scrutinize the list of attendees. You don't have to be at every meeting to be important. But when you must have a meeting, always run it well. When I began a new job not long ago, I decided to hold a meeting with my direct reports. I published a clear agenda with specific time allocations and then watched as my direct reports went over time by hours and presented thoroughly confusing information!

When the meeting concluded, I gave them an earful and told them they had better improve their preparation and timeliness – they had wasted my time and valuable time to our shareholders.

The next meeting was better but still below

my standards, and I once again dressed them down. I decided to institute the 'Two-Chart Rule'. No one could come to the meeting with more than two charts on their subject. They were forced to really consider what they put on those two charts.

At our first meeting under the Two-Chart Rule, one person did attempt to put up a third chart. As he clicked it on to the screen, I asked him to sit down. He protested, of course, saying, 'This is important!' I simply said, 'I am sure it is, but not today, Chief! We all play by the rules. Your peers did what I asked, and I expect you to also.'

I never had a problem again. Try it sometime. When your colleagues learn to respect meetings, you can relax the rule and just insist that they stick to their allotted time. If you are supposed to be in a meeting at a certain time, make sure you are there on time. I can't tell you how often I have waited for executives who show up for a meeting five or ten minutes late. Some even more. How stupid.

I have witnessed one executive who was so incensed by tardy arrivals at her staff meetings that she had a lock installed on the conference

room door. At the time the meeting was sched-
uled to start, she bolted the door and anyone
coming late was forced to knock to get in. Late
arrivals were thoroughly embarrassed, and there
were never repeat performances! I love it!

If you are travelling, get up on time. 'I over-
slept' doesn't cut it. I always pack a travel alarm,
plus I use the alarm in the room, and I order a
wake-up call. Paranoia? Nope, I just want to
get to where I'm going on time.

One of the biggest mistakes you can make is to
turn up late for a large-scale meeting. You know
the kind of meeting I'm talking about: your boss
is there, your boss's boss is there. You can't just
slip in late. Conference room doors always rattle
to announce a late arrival. Everyone in the audience turns around; everyone notices. Regardless
of whether or not you had a drop to drink the
night before, most people will assume you were
out late partying. Set three alarms if you have to,
or have a friend call you at an arranged time as an
added safety net. Get up on time and show up on
time. No one needs to get a bad reputation when
a little preparation is all it takes to be on time.

Answer Your Own Phone

When your phone rings, answer it. I love these people who have all their calls screened or just let the calls go to voicemail. What a colossal waste of time. By the time you check with your assistant or review your voicemails and call people back, you've spent two or three times more time and effort than you would have if you had just answered your phone.

People are pleasantly surprised when a senior executive actually answers his or her own phone. To me it's just an outward sign that says, 'Hey, I am open for business!' and 'I am ready to help.'

Of course you will get pesky salespeople occasionally, but I am okay with this – everybody has a job to do. I usually give them about thirty seconds to win me over, and if they don't, I politely thank them and move on.

You never know how valuable that call you just ignored might have been.

Don't Pad Your Expenses

Only claim your legitimate expenses; not one penny more. Know your company's policy on reimbursement and stay within the guidelines.

I watched a close friend ushered out of a company when he was found to be cheating on his expense report. He lost a very good job over a small amount of money. Worse than that, though, he lost his reputation, and he will never recover from that.

If a company sends in auditors to review expense reports (which they do from time to time), you want to be lily-white. Auditors are very good at what they do, and you don't want to be on the wrong side of an inquiry.

Expense claims are meant to keep you whole, not get you ahead.

RULE 24

Prepare for Plane Trips

As you move up inside a big company, it's more than likely that you will be required to travel extensively. Avoid the trap of acting like a tourist – mindlessly boarding the plane and spending the entire flight watching movies or reading airport novels.

Plane time can be quiet time: time that can be used very effectively if you plan for it. Make sure your planning is sensible, or don't bother planning at all. For example, if you are tired, plan a short nap, leave a bit of time to read part of a book or magazine, and then use the rest of the flight time to work. You will be able to rip through work very quickly without being disturbed.

Planes are tight on space these days, so

organize your work before you get on board. Don't waste valuable time fumbling around in tight quarters. I always prepare a work folder in advance and pack it in my briefcase so I can access it easily during the flight. It usually contains important reading material on things I need time to think about. If you are flying economy class, forget your PC: there simply isn't enough room to work. But you can still read and do some pen-and-paper work that will make a difference. I also find that the process of organizing my work in preparation for a trip has the effect of giving me a goal to achieve during the flight, which isn't a bad thing.

At the beginning of a flight, always introduce yourself to your seat mates: not to be nice, but to find out what they do for a living. The last thing you want to do is to be seated next to a competitor or a client with sensitive information on clear display. It is shocking how often it happens. I have heard many stories about this over the years, and I am telling you that most people you expose information to will sit back quietly and soak up as much competitive knowledge as possible without you even knowing. You are an absolute fool if you are not very guarded about the work you do during a flight. Same goes for mobile phones in public places. Don't make it easy for your competitors.

You must learn to sleep on planes – particularly on overnight flights, which are common for many executives and aspiring executives today. If you struggle with this, see your doctor and figure out a way to sleep. When you get off an overnight flight, you are expected to go straight to work. Okay, maybe a quick shower first. Taking a day to recover shows a lack of fortitude. You can't do it, because no one else does.

And don't go into the office and whine about being tired all day. Stay focused on the job and forget fatigue. Mind over matter has worked for me for years. If that starts to fail, grab a coffee. Smile and be strong.

RULE 25

You Are On Your Own, Baby!

Most companies do not make a practice of managing an individual's career. So, the responsibility for manoeuvering your way toward the top belongs to you. First, you must study the organization you work for and calculate the best next career move for you. Then you need to position yourself to get that job.

Generally, paths to the top are fairly clear. Take a look at the top executives in your company today and investigate their movements. The past is a precursor of the future. Did they run a particular division or business unit on their way to the top? Is there a pattern for success that emerges? If so, consider moving in a similar direction. If not, take an educated guess about the right direction.

For me, the path to the top has always been

clear: inside any multi-national corporation, you have to formulate your own plan to get to where you want to go, you have to deliver results, and you need to have a minimal number of corporate enemies. Figure out your path and make it happen. You have to do it yourself – no one will do it for you!

RULE 26

Take the Best Job

Many will disagree with me on this, but here goes. . .

Never go for the money – always go for the best job. The two are not necessarily linked. The best job is the one that will give you the skills and exposure you need to move swiftly.

I have few regrets about the moves I have made, but I do wish I could get one particular moment back. Early in my career I was offered a position working directly for the vice president of sales of a world-class consumer-products company. This was a fantastic job through which many of the company's leaders had passed on their way to the top. It was an impressive company and I would have been working for a brilliant guy who was positioned to move ahead quickly (that is, out of my way!). This job had it all, but it paid 15 percent less than my current job. I turned it down because of money, and that was stupid. I made a decision over a couple of thousand dollars! Spread over a career, it was nothing.

I watched the person who took the job flourish and move quickly – more quickly than me. Ouch. I caught up, but I lost time, and that will forever nag at me. I recovered, but I had learned a big lesson. Awesome spots in companies are rare. The money will come soon enough. Think long-term.

Never take a job that has 'special' in the title. It is corporate code for 'I am on my way out.' Think about it. Corporations spend huge amounts of time promoting teams and teamwork, and now they suddenly declare someone to be *special*?

Special is not good in most companies.

Keep an eye on the newspapers following a company reorganization. You will find a few people who are suddenly 'special'.

RULE 27

Choose Your Employer Carefully

There are companies out there that only promote from within their own ranks. This means that to get to the top, you must start at the bottom and work your way up. I used to work for a company like this, and in that type of environment, patience was king; on the upside, I never faced external competition.

Personally, this environment has never worked for me, as I like outside experience. I think you learn more through diverse experiences; I also think you get a broader perspective from working for multiple employers. But the point here is to choose your employer carefully. If you need a lot of change to stay motivated, a 'promote from within' culture won't suit you.

Few candidates do much during the interview process to try to understand the culture and working environment of a prospective employer. This should be of equal importance to the job title and compensation that is offered. Ask about it. Make it your mission to find out before you accept an offer and before it is too late.

At ACNielsen in Australia, our human resources team has produced a document that describes the ACNielsen employment experience – this is given to all candidates. This document tells the brutal truth, and to me is a clear best-demonstrated practice. We decided to do this because I didn't want to hire people who wouldn't fit in. It's too costly. Put the facts on the table. Everyone will benefit from this approach.

There are lots of choices out there. Pick the one that works best for you. Make an informed decision.

RULE 28

Ask for a Performance Review

Early in your career, in most companies, you will be given routine performance reviews. These are important. Even if you don't agree with the review, or some of it, sit back and realize that you need to deal with the perception you have created. For example, you may be a person who does a great deal of work at home in the evening, yet the perception is that you always leave the office early and are not working as hard as your colleagues. Talk it through with your boss and sort out a solution that will change the perception. Perceptions can kill your career!

Now for the bad news. As you get to senior levels in most corporations, you probably won't be given performance reviews willingly. This is yet another case of managers adhering to the principle of 'Do as I say, not as I do.' They will insist that reviews get done in the lower ranks, but they won't find time to conduct them with their own direct reports.

Not to worry. First, ask for one. You will probably get one. If not, ask your boss to lunch and talk to him or her about your strengths and weaknesses. Even if your boss is non-confrontational, you will undoubtedly hear a few things you can work on. Imagine if you are doing things that drive your boss or your colleagues crazy and you aren't even aware of them! This happens far too often, believe me.

The simplest way to find out is to take a chance and *ask* the question. Once you open that door, you may indeed get some surprising feedback. Accept whatever your boss tells you graciously – even if it hurts – and think about how you can work on any problems you now know about.

RULE 29

Do It by the Book

Business ethics have never been more front and centre than they are right now. And it's easy to understand why: consider the collapse of Enron, the disaster at WorldCom and the spate of very public dismissals of CEOs of large companies.

Honesty, integrity and ethics are a vital part of business and life. Never be tempted by an 'opportunity' that might cause a breach in these areas in your own chase for personal gain or record profits. It's flat-out wrong – and you will get caught.

Consider the lives of the well-intentioned staff that might lose their jobs because of a decision you make, not to mention your accountability to shareholders. And if that's not incentive enough, contemplate the price you will pay personally: criminal proceedings, no more 'big' jobs, and a life lived out in embarrassing exile.

Companies can implement expensive compliance systems as much as they like, but really, the only effective method by which corporate ethics can be employed is through the actions of each individual.

You can win and be rewarded by working hard and smart. Do it by the book: no excuses.

RULE 30

Embrace Change

Getting to the top requires courage. Never fear change. If you do not change, you will not grow. If you do not grow, you will not make it very far in any organization.

If you have been in your current job for two years or more, it is time to change. You should really start marketing yourself for your next job at the eighteen-month mark. You should assume that the process of landing your next job may take six months, possibly more. You will need persistence and patience.

Let your boss know you want a change and why. No one will find that threatening. Use the human resources department. Ask them to help you with your career. Believe me, they will help if they are any good.

Recently a very senior manager who worked in my organization approached his boss and me. He calmly described to us how he saw his own situation. He was positive and upbeat, and he explained how he had been in his current job for two years, performed well, and thought he was likely to be a candidate for his boss's job at some point. But, he said, his boss had been in his job for less than a year and was not likely to move soon. He proposed that he be moved to a similar job in a different country for two years with a likely return to his home country following this assignment. The experience would enable him to return with a greater skill set under his belt. It made sense to me, and that's what we did. This probably would not have happened without his initiative. Don't sit back and wait: you snooze, you lose!

Relish change. Relish new assignments and challenges. Once you truly believe change is good, you will seek it out on all occasions. You will set yourself apart.

Most big companies have an established system that allows employees to see internal employment opportunities across all divisions and in all locations. Postings can be a great way to spot an opportunity for advancement, but proceed with caution:

- **Never apply for a job** that you haven't first discussed with your boss. Amazingly, in big companies, people commonly apply for new positions without their boss's knowledge or support. This is a big no-no. You are going it alone unless your boss is in the boat with you.

- **If the opportunity is a good one** and you are qualified, chances are your boss will support you. If he or she is not supportive, find out why. Have a discussion. Discover the truth.

- **Be prepared for the question** a good boss will ask: 'If you take this opportunity, who will I fill your position with?' It will be easier for your boss to support your move if a clear successor is available. Have an answer ready for this question.

- **Don't apply for jobs** you aren't qualified for. You are not going to go from a middle-management role to a country managing director overnight. Careers are built on progression. It is good to dream, but do it privately.

Be proactive and seek opportunities. Job postings can be a great source of information. Use the system to your advantage.

RULE 31

Resign the Right Way

The process of tendering your resignation with
your employer must be as well thought out as
any other step you take in your career. You must
ensure that you keep your options open – you
may want to return one day; and you must
make sure you leave with your boss supporting
you – not out to get you. The world is a small
place; you want to find welcome signs on all
doors.

What should you think about?

- **First, as I have said earlier,** never surprise your boss. If you are getting close
  to accepting a position with another
  company, let your boss know in private.

* **Your boss will appreciate** the fact that it is not a done deal and that he or she may still have options. Don't be emotional, and don't appear to be demanding 'Match the offer or I'll go.' You will not win an extortion game, and you will severely undermine your current and future credibility.

* **Never resign via e-mail** or a letter. Sounds stupid? It is, but it happens. This is the quickest road to the 'Not Welcome Back' sign.

* **Don't resign when your boss** is about to leave town on business or vacation: Your boss will be unimpressed by your timing ... see 'Not Welcome Back' sign, above.

* **At an appropriate time** – after you have told your boss in person – send your boss an official resignation letter thanking him or her profusely for the work experience you have gained. Don't talk about your reasons for leaving: it might make you feel better, but it will

do nothing to enhance your situation, so don't waste the ink.

- **Stay true to your word** in regard to confidentiality. Don't take anything from your office that you do not have a right to. If you don't know, ask – or be prepared for possible litigation.

- **Be flexible about** your departure date. If they need you a bit longer, be accommodating.

- **Re-read your employment contract,** or any other agreements you may have with your current employer, before you resign. Expect that your employer will enforce provisions that favour them. Never expect that they will walk away from provisions that protect their business – even if they are your friends. They're not stupid.

- **If you are leaving** to join a direct competitor, be prepared for an immediate exit. Do as you are asked in a co-operative manner.

- **Never tell colleagues** you are looking for a new job. You will only be placing them in an awkward position. When you resign, a smart boss will ask when you started looking around and possibly who else knew.

- **Spend hours preparing** for your resignation. The world is small, careers are short and situations are fluid. You may want to rejoin a company you are now leaving further down the track, or work again for a manager who has moved on. A little planning and common sense will go a long, long way.

I made a whopper of a mistake when I resigned from a position in my late twenties. I am still, to this day, haunted by my own stupidity. At the time I was working in a start-up division of a global company. Business was not going well at the time and rumours of our division being closed were alive and well. The CEO called me into his office and, completely out of the blue, gave me a battlefield promotion to managing director – effectively in charge of running half the division! The trouble was, I was about to get a job offer from a start-up company in Boston. Great job. Great pay. Great location. But while I was in his office, my brain went on holiday. He continued to tell me about the promotion, but I heard little of what he said. I was stupid, young and confused.

I left his office not having said yes or no to the promotion. To my surprise, an hour later an announcement was made about my promotion. I went home sweating. The following day I walked into the office to a chorus of congratulations. But I wanted the other job, and I resigned three days later. When I told the CEO, he exploded; he told me to leave the building within thirty minutes or he would have security throw me out, and I am quite sure he meant it.

This was a classic rookie mistake. I should have come clean in our initial meeting. I flat-out embarrassed him. What a bonehead play. It was the mistake of all mistakes.

Make resigning a professional event, not amateur hour.

RULE 32

One Kick at the Can

When you change jobs or are promoted, you will be presented with a new compensation structure. This may include a base salary, bonus, car, long-term incentives, stock options and so on. Review the offer carefully and with immense realism. Most people don't double their income overnight. Greed can be good or stupid.

Intelligent executives will review an offer with the understanding that what is in front of them is pretty close to a final offer. Dumb executives will believe they should ask for the moon.

It has always been my belief that you get 'one kick at the can'. Consider any offer prag-matically and pick a couple of things that you would like to modestly amend. Present your suggestions with great humility and expect that you will have to compromise.

If you ask for too much or appear too demanding, you run the risk of damaging your relationship with a new employer at the outset. And you may never recover! Bad move.

If you want to score points, ask for your *variable* compensation to be inflated. Employers love this: It generally signals that you are honest and confident. From their point of view, it is risk-free. If you are very successful, they pay you a lot. If not, they don't pay. Go for the increase in stock options or other performance-based incentives. Base salary is the toughest and most dangerous item to negotiate. Be realistic.

I have personally pulled back two offers when the negotiation process got stupid. No way do I need the headache. The world is filled with great people; I want to employ people who are realistic and smart.

So remember, you only get one kick at the can.

RULE 33

Befriend Your
Legal Counsel

It is a very good idea to get to know your internal legal counsel. These men and women can be your 'friends'; they can really keep you and the company you work for out of the soup.

If you are going to terminate someone, check with them.

If you are doing a deal with a client, check with them.

If a client is breaching a contract, check with them.

If you are meeting with a competitor, check with them.

If you are signing any documents commit-

ting the company you work for to anything —
check with them.

Invest time with your legal counsel up front
and it will save you from big headaches —
potentially the career-destroying type — further
down the track.

Consider what happened to 'Bob.' Bob was
assigned to manage a business for his company
in one of its important markets in the United
States. The business had maintained a strong
position in this market for years, but had
recently been losing share to a creative and
aggressive new competitor. The company had
replaced the former general manager with Bob
because the former GM had not adapted to the
new competitive situation.

Bob arrived committed to making changes,
and making them fast. One of his first steps
was to call together his marketing team to
review the product line and pricing. Bob
quickly saw which of their products were suf-
fering the greatest losses to competition. He
devised a plan to price and market those products differently and directed the marketing
team to implement his plan immediately.

Bob monitored activities daily; the plan was working. Competitive losses came to an almost complete halt. Bob was quite pleased.

Then Bob received service of a formal legal document. The competitor had sued his company for violation of competition laws.

Bob was called to a meeting with his boss and the company's general counsel. The GC told Bob that none of the company's lawyers seemed to know anything about Bob's plan. Bob told him that it never occurred to him to talk to the lawyers; he was only adjusting his marketing to allow the company to compete more effectively.

The GC explained to Bob that while his intentions may have been good, his plan was not. Most of the practices Bob had adopted were very questionable, if not outright unlawful. The company would have a hard time defending Bob's actions. Moreover, the GC explained that had Bob checked with the lawyers, they would have shown him how to achieve his objectives within legal boundaries, just as they had addressed similar problems several times in the past.

The company spent three years in litigation, incurring legal fees and spending countless management hours in meetings and depositions. They eventually settled the case for a hefty sum, money that effectively funded the competitor's efforts against the company. Their competitor remains firmly entrenched in that market today. Bob is no longer with that company.

Legal counsel exists in companies to help, not to slow things down. Educate them on your area of business and the challenges you are facing. Establish a working relationship with your in-house legal team as early as possible, and include them as an active part of your team. You will reap big benefits and avoid making mistakes fatal to your company and career. The world has become a very litigious place to live in during the past decade or so; the corporate world has become obsessed with litigation. It has been my experience that this trend inside corporations is not being driven by the much maligned legal community but rather by businessmen and women working every angle possible to find a way to improve business results.

If you are a business leader, consider the immediate costs of litigation versus the possible outcome of a distant lucrative settlement. Total victories tend to be few and far between, and the cost of litigation is very high indeed. Most people will want to achieve a business solution rather than go to court.

It's expensive to have lawyers doing their job, and this is just one of the 'hard' costs. You have to weigh in the 'soft' costs, too, such as the time you will need to spend away from your business. Never underestimate the damage this can cause.

Carefully think through any situation before you commit to litigation. It can take years to work things through court systems (regardless of where you are in the world), and once you start, it is hard to disengage. Disengagement is sometimes a very prudent path to take, but it feels like you've lost.

Lawyers will usually give you the facts as they see them *and* your chances of actually winning. Don't take this personally, and don't let your emotions get the best of you: Make a rational and objective business decision. Don't spend all your time in court at the expense of attending to your business.

RULE 34

Prepare for Your Big Presentation

In a large company, you get very few chances to present to the top one or two people. If you get one, make sure you are really ready. Synthesize your message and minimize the number of charts. 'Dumb down' the information. Remember, the top execs are usually a mile wide and an inch deep: they are paid to know something about everything, but in most cases they won't have all the details.

The quickest way to lose an audience is to present things they don't understand. Find out what they are familiar with and interested in. Keep your visuals clear, uncluttered and simple. A short presentation has more of an impact than a long one.

I have found that the average CEO has the attention span of a ten-year-old. Give them an interesting, simple story, and they will listen and enjoy it. Give them a technical, boring presentation, and you will lose them every time.

Pay attention to your audience when you are presenting. If they are signaling you to speed up, speed up. Give them what they want while you deliver your message.

And when you are done, thank them for their time. CEOs like to be thanked. It doesn't happen much at the top.

Lots of careers get killed by bad presentations. Preparation and knowing your audience are king!

Remember:

- **Invest time in preparation.**
- **Know your audience.**
- **Simplify your material and messages.**
- **Make recommendations and conclusions.**
- **Summarize when you are closing.**
- **Finish your presentation on time.**
- **Say 'thank you' to your audience.**

RULE 35

Surround Yourself with Talent

We are all good at some things and lousy at others. Assess what you don't do well, and as you build your organization or team, surround yourself with people who balance your weak areas. Never fear finding and hiring someone better than you. The better they are, the better you will look.

Hire people who will be loyal to you and share your values. Hire people with energy and passion. Only hire people with positive attitudes. Fire anyone with a bad attitude. They are organizational cancer and need to be cut out before their negativity spreads.

Make sure everyone in your organization knows their roles, and give them freedom to execute their plans. Don't write plans for people who work for you. Let them write their own plans and then work with them in the editing and refining stage. You will quickly learn who your best managers are: they will be the ones who write the best plans and probably the ones who are most eager to get your feedback and fine-tune their efforts. Make no mistake, there is a strong correlation between sloppy plans and poor results.

Diverse skill sets are beautiful! Orchestrate them to work as one and you have a killer combination. Companies are littered with people who think it is a sign of weakness to delegate work. These are usually people who are either control freaks or scared to death that someone will perceive them to be less valuable to the organization if others can do some of their work.

Nothing could be further from the truth. Organizations expect managers to organize and delegate work downward. Similarly, employees further down the food chain expect work and decisions to be delegated to them. They become frustrated when all the decisions and interesting work occurs above their head. They want to be challenged and they want to feel relevant.

Never be hesitant about delegating work. Push downward what is appropriate and hold on to what you need to do. If you can delegate work effectively, you will be perceived as a solid manager by those above you and those below you.

RULE 36

Listen for What
You Don't Hear

One tough part about rising up the corporate food chain is that the further up you go, the more sanitized the information you receive becomes. In short, people want to stay on safe ground, so they often package up or water down the truth. Listen carefully and watch their body language. Probe with questions when you sense that something might be wrong. Or do what I do sometimes: come straight out and ask for the truth. This usually disarms people and they will spill the whole truth because you have already supplied a safety net.

Listening sounds easy, but it is a difficult sport – a learned skill. Sitting quietly without interjecting with an opinion or a thought is not what we are taught to do. We are taught to participate actively and often.

Learn to listen. Good listeners get to the truth. The truth allows for good decisions. Good decisions will move your career. Along with listening, become a good communicator. Tell the truth and never 'Santa Claus' poor results. If you are not making your numbers, admit it and put a plan in place – a visible one – to get back on course. Forget the ho-ho-ho. No one cares. Winners find a way to win. Losers talk about how well they did while they were missing their numbers. Good managers see right through that.

The world is demanding short-term results, so you should expect enormous pressure to deliver *this year's* results. Long-term thinking is a part of your job, but if you don't deliver the bacon this year, somebody else will be sitting in your chair next year.

I have yet to see an announcement of a promotion that reads: 'Sally has missed her numbers for two consecutive years, but she has a great long-term plan for the division and I am promoting her.'

You deliver results – and deliver them fast – you get promoted. Really simple.

RULE 37

Coach Your Team

Phil Jackson, formerly the head coach of the Los Angeles Lakers, is, to me, one of the best coaches in any sport of all time. I've never met him, but I've followed his career for years. Phil has coached multiple championship teams now, with both the Lakers and the Chicago Bulls. He has the ability to 'stir the drink': he can take great players and fit them together like a craftsman. He fits players like bad-boy Dennis Rodman in with superstar Michael Jordan and role-player Scottie Pippen. Very few complain because he works his agenda beautifully. It seems to me his best skill is his ability to balance egos, skills, talents and weaknesses quietly and calmly. With Phil, it's definitely not about him. It's about the team performing and winning. And can he handle the pressure!

The role of a professional sports coach is akin to that of a manager in a corporation:

- **They must be able to spot talent and recruit it.**
- **They must blend talent and balance their team's strengths and weaknesses.**
- **They have to tell people what their roles are.**
- **They must motivate their team to achieve lofty goals.**
- **They are not allowed to have a bad day.**
- **They have to eliminate low performers.**
- **They only get to keep their jobs as long as they are winning.**

Now you know why coaches and athletes are often brought into corporations to deliver motivational speeches. Sport is a business: a very visible business, with issues and opportunities that are identical to those of any corporation.

———————

How well are you coaching your team?

The new millennium has seen a change in what we want from our leaders. Gone are the days of the tyrant boss: the screamers and the shouters, the blamers and the embarrassers.

Today's successful leaders are cool and collected. They always give the appearance of being in control. They listen calmly and offer leadership in a methodical and professional way. They empathize with employees. They work to explain their actions and decisions to gain 'buy-in'.

Today's manager needs to be inclusive in the decision-making process. All opinions should be welcome. 'You may not like my decision, but you will have input' will always win over the troops. Being inclusive motivates staff.

People naturally want their opinions heard. They want to feel that they are part of the process and in the loop. People who are excluded from decisions feel less important and therefore less motivated. A very good measure for understanding how you are doing as a business manager is how many of your direct reports unexpectedly resign each year. I have never lost more than one in a year, and in many years I have lost none at all.

If your staff is happy, you are doing your job. People don't often leave jobs – and, in particular, bosses – that they like. Treat people the right way and you will have disciples for life.

RULE 38

Take Care of Your Best People

I learned this from the chairman of a very successful company whom I worked for earlier in my career. When he first arrived at the company, he organized a meeting of the top ten managers and laid out his plans and vision for the future. Following the meeting, he invited us to join him for dinner at a local restaurant. His new assistant had arranged everything.

We walked into the restaurant and everyone immediately noticed the tired decor. I heard him mutter something under his breath. I asked him what was wrong, and he said that you never, ever, take the top people in your company to a lousy restaurant. Period. He said:

'You have to take the best care of your best people.'

It's about more than restaurants, it's about *everything* you do. You have to look after your high-fliers at a different level. The senior people feed the tribe, and you need to treat them like gold.

He was right – as he almost always was.

RULE 39

You Can't Say 'Thank You' Enough

People want to be thanked for their work. Studies I have read suggest that it is often just as important as the pay they receive. It is such a simple and easy thing to do, but it doesn't happen enough in most companies.

'Thank you' can be delivered in many ways. The most sincere way is to shake someone's hand, look them in the eye, and say 'Thank you' with sincerity – it certainly has the most impact. A spoken thank-you delivered personally to a large number of people or a team is also effective.

One of the oldest methods that still works – and seems to be making a comeback with younger managers – is a handwritten thank-you note. Simple, quick, and sincere.

Sorry, but saying "thank you" via a mass e-mail simply stinks. It comes across as superficial and trite: You can't touch it or feel it! Delete it from your game. Or if you are forced to use it, follow up with a phone call to have a little more impact.

Whenever you can, publicly credit 'the team'. Every senior manager loves to use the words *team* and *teamwork*. These words resonate in the corridors of all corporations. Resist the urge to take individual credit.

People feel good about teams that succeed. You may be the best player on the team, but always remain humble. Praise the team – talk about everyone's contributions and downplay your own role, even if it was very significant.

Listen to what a good coach says after a victory: 'The team played well; they executed the game plan.' Or, 'I really want to thank the fans for their loyalty.' Or, 'I would like to thank the owners for inviting me along for the ride.' They compliment everyone except themselves. They know that people are smart enough to realize – without being told – that the coach

was integral to the team's success. Win cham-
pionships and you will get noticed. Credit the
team and you will be loved.

RULE 40

Beat Stress Back

Resist the urge to fall into your job every day without strolling out on to 'the balcony' for an hour at least once a week. The balcony is a place where you can look down on everything that's happening in your life. The balcony is a place where you can think about your business and what could be done to grow it without the intrusion of daily distractions. The balcony is a 'thinking game'; finding the time and making it a priority can be challenging, but it is critical. All good leaders do it.

Most senior executives I know routinely make time to have a high-level thought session about their business. Most have a ritual that drives this event: Some do it while taking a morning or evening walk; others while they're alone in a café with a coffee.

For me, it's usually on a Friday night. The office tends to clear out fairly early, so it's nice and quiet. I take the opportunity to spend some time silently thinking about the week that has just passed and, of course, about the bigger picture of the business and where it's going. I write things down and I review ideas every week. Yes, on Fridays I'm tired and I want to go home, but finding this balcony makes me better than my competitors.

I have heard a great story that has been attributed to Bill Gates. Apparently Gates was once asked what he was doing (when he was apparently doing nothing). He replied: 'I'm thinking, you should try it.' We can't all be as smart (or as rich!) as Bill Gates, but we can learn from the Microsoft Man.

It has been said before that stress comes from doing things you don't like, and I think that's true. I also think that stress can come from the sheer volume of work people are expected to do. In most corporations today, every employee has a full plate of work in front of them. And as I have mentioned earlier, you either keep up or you get kicked out. Throw in the added pressure of a significant other or family, and most people will tell you they feel stressed. It sounds bleak, but it certainly has been this way for some time and it's unlikely to change. So, like everything else in life, you have to stare stress right in the face and deal with it.

Some of the things I do when I feel stressed that you might like to consider include:

- **Taking a five-minute walk outside or even around the office. Simple, but it really helps.**
- **Acknowledge that stress usually comes in bursts and that the situation will calm down. Keep reminding yourself of this.**
- **'Swiss cheese' the situation that's bothering you. That is, attack a problem by poking holes in it and solving pieces of the problem one step at a time instead of trying to attack the whole problem at once.**

- Write down on paper everything that is causing you stress. Sometimes when you put them on paper they don't seem as terrible.
- Smile – it just always feels good to smile.
- Visit a comedy club – nothing beats stress back better than a good laugh.

You need to be honest with yourself. If you are continually stressed out by your job, ask yourself if you are in the right job. Everyone should do things they enjoy. You do things that you enjoy well (golf is an exception to this rule for me). Life is just too short to be tortured every day.

I have had several close friends who scaled to the near top of major corporations and gave it all up simply because of the stress. For one colleague, the stress spilled over to his personal life, and he lost his wife and kids. He got out too late. The other got out in time. Both are now happy and making good livings in more relaxed environments. Classic cases of square pegs in round holes. If it's not a fit, it's not a fit.

RULE 41

Don't Get Too
Full of Yourself

As my mother would say, 'Don't get too big for your breeches.'

If you have a company event, help set up beforehand. If you are at a company picnic, serve the sandwiches or pick up the rubbish. Little actions get noticed.

I was reminded of this at an all-company meeting last year when I was due to present our year-to-date results to 650 people. I arrived an hour early to check out the venue and watched as people were scrambling to get ready. A young woman was putting agendas on each chair in the theatre. I grabbed half of her pile and helped her distribute them. Afterwards, she approached me and said, 'I've never seen a

CEO do that.' I was a bit amazed, and the comment made me feel great. I found out later that word had spread throughout the organization about me being a normal guy who pitches in to help.

The message is simple: don't get too full of yourself.

Understand People Differences

The world is made up of lots of different kinds of people. Getting a handle on some of the traits or characteristics of the larger groups can be valuable in terms of structuring a team or a company to get the most out of your colleagues.

Much has been written in recent years about various groups of people and the characteristics that define them. It has been my own experience that there are three main different groups: Baby Boomers, Generation X, and Generation Y. Broadly speaking, here is what I see.

Baby Boomers is the group that most people define as being the generation born between the end of World War II and the mid-1960s;

they form a large percentage of today's population worldwide. The Boomers are an employer's dream: They love to work. Boomers are willing to work long and hard, and most have the goal of retiring comfortably at a reasonable age. Boomers are family-oriented and firmly believe in education for themselves and their family. They are confident and focused on the future, but they also have a healthy fear of the future.

What can you learn from this? Lots. Baby Boomers will continue to work long and hard if they are properly motivated. Incentive schemes generally work well, as they want to quickly amass a retirement nest egg. This group gets rattled quickly when business goes through a rough patch, because they are older than the other two generations coming through and so have a greater fear of losing their jobs. I view Baby Boomers as a real workhorse segment of the population – a great group to employ.

Generation Xers were born between the mid-1960s and the very early 1980s and are really hitting their stride in the workforce right now. They are an interesting group and very,

very different from the Boomers. They love technology and love to experiment. They are self-confident and live for today. Generation Xers expect to be paid very well and will happily job-hop to earn more money. They expect work to be fun and exciting, as well as comfortable, but they are not willing to work incredibly long hours, even when offered special incentives.

Obviously this will be a growing sector of the workforce as the Baby Boomers retire, and this poses a risk for many companies. This group just won't work the same hours as the Baby Boomers and isn't easily intimidated or afraid of being fired. Gen Xers value their time off enormously and are probably a healthier lifestyle group than the Boomers, because they have a better mix of work and leisure time. This is, however, a lousy characteristic from an employer's point of view. As I have stated earlier in this book, time on the job counts.

The Generation Y group – those born since the very early 1980s – has grown up in pretty good times. They tend to think more globally than the other two groups and are willing and excited about traveling to locations distant from their homes. They devour information from television, radio, the Internet, books, magazines, and newspapers. Most are or will be very well educated. This group will probably be technological geniuses, and like the Xers, they will expect big incomes. The jury is still out on how long and hard they will be willing to work.

I think Generation Y will thirst for overseas assignments but will become bored quite quickly on projects. Frequent rotations will be required to keep them active and interested. They are money hungry, and I also predict that they will spend money quickly. I wish I knew more about their work ethic: I hazard a guess that it will be high, as they will need money to sustain their spending habits.

There is nothing to fear from any of these groups. The point is that it's important to recognize these groups and, of course, individuals so that you can understand their needs and desires. The better you understand people and their differences, the better you will be able to motivate them effectively.

RULE 43

Hire Right, Fire Fast

The people you hire will make or break your career. People are the lifeblood of any organization. They invent, they improve, they handle client interface, and yes, sometimes they drive you crazy. Invest time in the hiring process to find the best people.

Start by really studying a candidate's résumé. What have they done? How often have they been promoted? Are they a job-hopper? Do they appear to have the skills you need? What are their outside interests? Prepare your personal-interview questions in advance, and make sure you direct the interview in a way that will ensure that you get answers to *all* of your questions. And definitely do reference checks; you never know what you might learn.

'Fast' can be difficult when it comes to firing. In most companies, you can fire someone quickly if they have done something really stupid such as steal or cheat; getting rid of someone who is only a poor performer can be more challenging. The process often involves written warnings, attempts to improve their results . . . it can take months. But if someone isn't cutting it, you need to take the necessary steps to sweep them out the door as quickly as you possibly can.

RULE 44

Succession Planning: Do It

Succession planning is about getting ready for the future, preparing for the inevitable. Succession planning is all about making sure you have Sally ready to plug into a job if John unplugs for a new job, or being prepared if either leaves the company or is promoted.

Good succession planning means you have options. Bad succession planning means you have an organization with no 'bench strength'. You will have limited options at a difficult time and your organization will struggle while you scramble. In turn, this also means a drop in productivity and diminished results – something no manager wants or can afford, and something shareholders will frown upon. You, personally, will be labelled as a poor planner.

Good companies and managers review their succession plans for key executives twice a year. This review process is important, but taking the action required to get ready for the inevitable is what really separates the men from the boys.

Do not over-complicate the process. Review your list of critical positions and determine, person by person, who fills the gap should that person leave the company. Focus on the spots where you have no clear successor; these are the points of vulnerability that you must address immediately. Fix those holes! Hire some new talent. Bring someone in from overseas, move someone from another division. Make sure you have a viable backup for every single critical position.

If you are not doing this already, start an organized process now. Discuss with your peers where successors are today on the 'ready' ladder. The process can be enlightening.

RULE 45

Never Grandstand

Grandstanders are people who make more out of a topic or issue than it deserves—often to the detriment of others, and always for personal gain.

You can only get away with grandstanding once (usually) in most companies. After that you will be labelled a self-serving loudmouth. There is a clear gap between being passionate about something and grandstanding. Passionate people truly believe in something and try to win others over with pure intentions. Grandstanders are simply trying to get ahead at the expense of others.

I once watched a brand manager stand in front of me and take me through a presentation on how great a new product launch had been. I sat in silence while he waxed lyrical about success after success. If I hadn't known my numbers, I would have believed this manager was a genius. When he was finished, I asked him one simple question: 'Am I nuts, or have we actually sold almost none of this product?' He looked befuddled, and he didn't last terribly long with the company after that.

Grandstanding is a quick way to lose supporters and fall out of the game. Make sure you don't do it.

Another pet peeve of mine are martyrs. Every company I have ever worked for has at least one martyr – and you can usually spot them pretty easily.

Martyrs always work incredibly long hours . . . and they let you know it. Martyrs always work weekends . . . and they let you know it. Martyrs solve all problems all by themselves . . . and they let you know it. Martyrs take flights at horribly inconvenient times . . . and they let you know it. Martyrs spend little time with their families . . . and they let you know it.

Don't be a martyr. Martyrs are see-through and shallow and won't get far in the corporate world.

RULE 46

Skip the Spin,
Tell the Truth

Corporations are littered with spin doctors at
all levels. Spin doctors don't exactly lie, but
they don't exactly tell the truth, either. It is
usually very easy to spot a spin doctor. They
are the person in front of the room explain-
ing away poor results or huge mistakes. They
will use words like *learning experience, great
team effort, the market shifted,* all the while
diverting attention from the fact that they
failed.

I have always hated excuses, and the managers on my team know better than to go down
this path. I would much rather hear the truth
and move on than listen to hours of psycho-
babble about what should have been. Psycho-

babble does not lead to better results. The truth and hard work do.

Spin doctors live at all levels of a company. Some of the best spin doctors are CEOs . . . but CEOs with a short tenure if things turn bad.

Maury Pagés, a former executive at Pepsi, is the best I have ever seen at shutting down spin doctors. Once during a presentation by a chief financial officer, I witnessed Maury asking the presenter to 'move on'. When he didn't, Maury got out of his seat and physically ripped up the CFO's charts. Pretty clear message. He was also famous for telling spin doctors, 'I asked you what time it was, not how to build a watch.' Another clear signal.

Seasoned executives can smell spin. You won't score points by trying to mask a difficult situation, so don't bother. Lay out the truth so your organization can deal with it effectively.

RULE 47

Take Intelligent Risks and Admit When You Fail

All companies hate big failures, but all companies like executives who are not afraid to take a risk.

Taking a risk inside a company is little more than making an intelligent bet. The secret is never to have a spectacular or public failure. For every one good idea, there are hundreds of failures. Most companies realize that the quest for that one elegant solution is worth ninety-nine failures. As long as the idea was a good one, the plan was thorough, management knew in advance what was happening and the failure was not catastrophic, you have little risk of damaging your career.

Risk and failure are tolerated and sometimes

rewarded inside companies. Push the envelope whenever you can. One exceptional innovation will outweigh many, many failures. The quickest way to defuse a mistake in a major corporation is to accept accountability. Admit failure with your chin held high. You will appear strong and self-confident. You will also be perceived as being team-oriented. Most of all, the mistake won't linger on publicly: there's no reason for it to do so when someone has claimed ownership. It is hard to blame someone when they have admitted they failed.

I have had only one disaster in my career. My team lost a large, prestigious client to a competitor. As soon as I was notified, I called our president and told him I made a mistake and offered my resignation. He laughed and said: 'No way.' He said the company had just made a multimillion-dollar investment in my education. No one leaves after that kind of investment.

There was no ridicule afterward and no political fallout. It would not be popular – or smart – to take shots at someone whom the president had forgiven, so no one did.

Admit mistakes and make sure your team understands that failure is a part of the game. While people and organizations are usually fairly forgiving when a mistake occurs and you admit to it, be very careful never to make the same mistake twice. People who do this are usually all done: They look really stupid, and their boss will be worrying that the third time is coming at any moment.

Trying new things and occasionally failing is part of life, and that's okay – just steer well clear of areas where you have experienced failure in the past unless you believe success is highly probable this time.

RULE 48

Never Write an E-mail Out of Anger

Get as mad as you want, but never, ever, write a note that assassinates another employee. It will happen (sometimes often) that someone will anger you to the boiling point and you will want to strike back at them . . . hard and fast.

Resist, resist, resist.

In the e-mail age we live in, it is too easy for a nasty note to be widely circulated. While your point may be correct, you will look out of control, possibly bitter, and maybe even spiteful. Stay cool.

Never forget how small the world really is. The person you assassinate today may come back to haunt you in the years to come. Win the battle without making a lifelong enemy.

RULE 49

Know Your Opponent

Study your competition. This is a lesson the great warriors of the past knew well. Regardless of whether it is a person or a company you are competing with, study their movements and learn their habits. Try to think the way they think. Anticipate their moves and get there before them with something better.

Don't be fooled by appearances and never underestimate a competitor. The world is full of people who have glossed over their competitors. David can still slay Goliath.

When you need to study a competitor, send a person or a group away on a 'mission'. Of course they should read everything they can on the company, but also have them use their own networks to find out more. For example, have them talk to former employees or clients; that's where the real learning is. Go one step further and task the individual or group with guessing what the competitor is thinking or what move they might be considering. This is what great generals have done in the past: anticipate their enemy's moves and then beat them to the target. Lots of books have compared the military with the business world; I think there are many, many similarities. Be a General!

RULE 50

Disarm Your Opponent

Inside a company it is always okay to disagree and express your opinions, as long as you do so in an appropriate manner.

Bill Moss – who is the banking-and-property-group head for Macquarie Bank in Australia – has taught me one of the best ways to get a different point of view across in a meeting of any size. When Bill wants to disagree, he always asks this question: 'Can I challenge that?' It is one of the most effective and disarming lines I have heard.

Of course the answer he receives is always 'Sure,' and this then opens the door for him to table a competing point of view in a very non-threatening manner.

I love it, and I am now using it regularly. You should, too.

RULE 51

Accept Politics

Office politics are a fact of corporate life, and the bigger the company you work for, the more complex and more ferocious the politics are. In an office situation, everyone is trying to get ahead and gain an advantage. Everyone has their own strategy, and this breeds politics. Some play dirty.

Realistically, you can expect that in most large corporations there will be around ten to fifteen people you will need to be cautious of. These are usually people who are more senior than you. You also have to watch out for some people at your own level, and maybe even the odd person who is below you, if they are 'big influencers'. Senior management listens to all of these people, so their opinions really do count. Stay on the right side of these people, or at the very least stay neutral with them.

I remember an interview a few years back, when a candidate told me he hated office politics and 'refused to play that game'. I didn't hire him because of that one comment. Politics do exist, plain and simple, so you can't bury your head and pretend they don't. Understand who the players are and set a personal strategy for how to deal with them effectively.

RULE 52

Leave Your Emotional Baggage at the Door

When you walk into work in the morning, leave your emotional baggage at the door. You are there to work and you need to be focused. If you need time off, take it. It's better to take a couple of days' vacation time than turn up at work distracted and grumpy. You will only make mistakes – and mistakes are seldom overlooked just because you are having a bad day or a bad week in your personal life.

And don't kid yourself about your workmates: Some will exploit your situation to their advantage. They will portray you as an emotional mess and out of control.

If you're not 100 percent, stay home. Better to sit out of the game than play and play badly.

RULE 53

Party, But Know
Your Limits

Socializing with colleagues can be motivational and allows you to gather information in a much more open and casual environment. Parties can be fun! I always make an effort to attend company gatherings. It is important to be seen and to let everyone know you enjoy time with your co-workers. The ability to get along, inspire — and be seen as a people person is good for your reputation.

When you attend company gatherings, go out and have a good time, of course, but watch how much you drink. Socialize, but be among the first to leave. It's been my experience that after a couple of hours of drinking, very little good occurs. Pack it in early, get your rest, and be at your best for the business meeting the next day. That's when you score the most points anyway! Never cultivate an image of being a playboy, playgirl or party animal. I have worked with several people who have justifiably earned reputations as playboys and party animals. After every meeting, they closed down the bar or were out on the prowl all night. I guess that's their call – until it inevitably spills over into work; then they are out of line. How? Well, how fresh are these people for meetings that start at 7:30 A.M.? Not very. Do you think they can contribute at 100 percent? Nope.

Playboys, playgirls, and party animals do not get promoted. Once you get this kind of reputation, you may never be able to lose it – and it will stop your career.

How about friendships? Straight up – having friends at work is not a great idea. I guess when you are young and first join a company the risk is fairly small. But as you progress through the ranks in an organization, especially when you begin to supervise staff, friendships become a massive complication. Think about it . . . will your friends be happy with you telling them what to do? If you are faced with laying off someone, can you make a clinical business decision if it involves friends? Would your friendship survive a termination? The list goes on and on. . .

Someone at a cocktail party recently asked me about my transition from North America to Australia. She said to me, 'Oh, you must have made a few friends at work.' She was a bit stunned when I said, 'No, I have no friends at work. I have acquaintances. Friends and work don't mix.'

Making friends at work is easy, but not smart.

RULE 54

You Won't Win Popularity Contests

Making decisions that are popular in a company is easy. Everyone wants to be popular. But get your head around one simple concept: The right decision is not always the most popular decision. Don't ever make the wrong decision just because it's easy. Always make the right decision, no matter how unpopular it may be.

The most unpopular decisions always involve people. And the more people these decisions involve, the worse it is. In my career there have been four times when I have had to make significant layoff or redundancy decisions that in total involved thousands of people – and, of course, their families. Developing the 'who stays' and 'who goes' list is nothing short of agony. Breaking the news to those who have to go is one notch worse. These kinds of decisions are necessary for companies to survive and flourish, but they are extremely difficult to make. And your popularity will take a beating.

If you're aiming for the top, it's best if you don't expect to be popular.

RULE 55

Be Discreet

Eileen Malloy, the United States Consul General in Sydney, Australia, once told me that one of the most challenging parts of her job is that she can never really relax. I asked, 'How come?' and she said she has to be on guard all the time because almost anything she says could end up in the newspaper, possibly in a very misconstrued manner.

Although it is often not as overt, the need for discretion is just as critical in business. You must carefully choose those people inside your company whom you trust. Rumour mills are a reality, and very few people are truly good at maintaining confidentiality. Don't risk any negative commentary by confiding in those you don't fully trust. It will inevitably come full circle and bite you on the backside.

I made the mistake once of telling a colleague in Canada that I was unhappy with the profit margins of a company we had recently bought. Twenty-four hours later, the CEO of that company called me – the story he had heard was that we were about to close his company down! How many people had bent the truth before he heard it?

Be smart about what you say and whom you say it to. Expect the worst, and let that drive your thinking and your comments.

RULE 56

It's Not All About You!

Last lesson in the book: Corporate life is not all about you. The corporation needs to do things to prosper – and sometimes just to survive. Your needs will seldom, if ever, be put ahead of the needs of the corporation. You are merely one small part of the equation, a piece of the machinery that makes things work.

Don't get to a point where you think you are more important than the corporation, because quite simply, *you are not*. You can be replaced. The company can find someone else who can do your job, and probably do it well.

Be realistic and you will be successful and happy.

EPILOGUE

So, now you have finished reading this book; that's great, but the true test is in how you *apply* the knowledge you have gained. Remember my advice in the introduction: the process of learning will accelerate your path to correct action, and taking correct action is what will get you ahead inside companies of any size at a faster pace. Find your own way to take action; the world needs better leaders.

A colleague of mine has a plaque above his desk that reads:

DWYPYWD

It stands for: *Do What You Promised You Would Do*.

These are certainly wise words to live by. If you always do what you promised you would do, not only is your boss likely to admire you for life, but your career will move forward in leaps and bounds.

Keep this book by your desk and flip through it once in a while. There are so many things you have to do right in order to succeed, so you will definitely benefit from an occasional review.

Work hard and smart, keep smiling, and enjoy your career, your life and your family. Good luck!

ACKNOWLEDGMENTS

I would like to acknowledge the many friends and colleagues who took time to contribute to my thinking for this book, especially Charlie Baker, Angie Benko, Todd Brant, Phil Chambers, Emmett Davis, Brian Goorjian, Shane Heal, Paul Lainis, Martin Lindstrom, Bob Livingston, Eileen Malloy, Frank Martell, Ted Marzilli, Andrew Michael, Laurence Michael, Nancy Michalowski, Bill Moss, John O'Keefe, Maury Pagés, Ed Riehl, Dawn Robertson, Donna Robertson-Hussin, Audrey Rosen and Steve Schmidt. Thank you all. Also a big thank-you to ACNielsen, a great company.

I would also like to thank the awesome people at HarperCollins, including Brian Murray, Knox Huston and Marion Maneker. A special thank-you to Ali Orman, who was the first to edit this manuscript in Sydney and really made a difference.

A great big sincere thanks to John Kench, who provided a connection for me to HarperCollins. An author needs connections!

Finally, personal thanks to my family – my wife, Sarah, and my kids, Zach, Abby, Nate, and Rebecca – for putting up with me during the chaotic time I spent writing this book and rewriting it to fit in to so many different countries.

What a fantastic experience!

ABOUT THE AUTHOR

TOM MARKERT is currently global chief marketing and client service officer with ACNielsen in New York. He has held leadership positions at Citicorp and Procter & Gamble as well as positions on the board of directors of the Australian professional basketball team, the Sydney Kings, and the American Chamber of Commerce in New South Wales, Australia. He lives in Connecticut.